The Truth About Bankruptcy
in Massachusetts

The Truth About Bankruptcy in Massachusetts

Peter M. Daigle, Esq.

ISBN: 1507779240
ISBN 13: 9781507779248
Library of Congress Control Number: 2015901905
Createspace Independent Publishing Platform,
North Charleston, South Carolina

Testimonials

"Peter Daigle and his staff were very professional and knowledgeable. They made me feel comfortable during a difficult time and followed through on each thing they said they would. I would highly recommend them to anyone."
—Kevin H.

"I can only tell you that Peter Daigle and his team are amazing, and all the people I have dealt with in his firm were an amazing, hardworking team. They were informative and answered every question and helped with all the strategies that I needed; they were there with advice and hard work to get it done. They are so easy to deal with from the receptionist to all the legal team. Peter was always there guiding his team, and I was getting done what I needed. I want to say this is rare in most firms. I promise anyone who is working

with Peter Daigle's law office will be satisfied with the professionalism and the outcome."
—Kathleen C.

"Great working with you. You are very helpful and knowledgeable of your job."
—Ed F.
"I wanted to take an opportunity to say how professional and reassuring you have been with me on my mother's case. You have returned calls promptly and have been very clear in explanations and laying out the next step."
—Helen B.

"Peter Daigle and his staff were very professional and knowledgeable. They made me feel comfortable during a difficult time and followed through on each thing they said they would. I would highly recommend them."

—Matthew W. "I am so glad attorney Daigle was the attorney to help me with the difficult decision to file Chapter 7. He was professional and competent, unlike some I saw at my hearing. The entire office staff was extremely helpful and available. I couldn't have made a better choice."
—Janet S.

Letter From the Author

If you're reading this book, the chances are that there has been a financial bump in the road for you or someone you know. It is nearly impossible to get through life unscathed. When I look around at those in my life, I see all sorts of unforeseen circumstances that have caused major life changes, whether through illness, divorce, job loss, or business loss.

My career as an attorney began where my previous one left off, as a real estate developer and general contractor who got caught in a down market. Despite all of the successes I had, it didn't end up the way I planned. It all happened to me—foreclosure, judgments, creditors, IRS. You name it. It could be happening to you. I've felt your pain. I've awoken at three in the morning worrying about how to deal with creditors; I've felt my pulse elevate every time the phone rang; I've been afraid to open my mail.

So with my fresh start, I went to law school and became a bankruptcy attorney, and it has changed my life. It is my turn to fight for you by using my professional skills and my real-world experience to get you a fresh start. I now spend my day counseling individuals and families on options based on their circumstances. In all cases, we come up with a plan. And with that plan, my clients feel empowered and rejuvenated—ready to take their lives back. Armed with a discharge in bankruptcy, they are able to start over with all of their possessions intact and their credit scores on the mend.

It all begins with knowledge to dispel the myths of bankruptcy, and that is the reason for this book. There is too much misinformation out there. You'll get it from your family, friends, and acquaintances and even overhear it in the grocery store. It's time to learn the truth about bankruptcy in Massachusetts.

I hope you read this book and feel empowered to make a change in your life.

Warmest regards,
Peter M. Daigle

Contents

Getting Started

Why file bankruptcy?

Maura was an elderly woman who had paid her bills on time all of her life, but she had begun to accumulate credit card debt to pay basic expenses when she was forced to give up her part-time job due to ill health. She only had her Social Security check each month. Now the monthly minimum payments were cutting into her budget to the point that she was unable to pay her monthly living expenses. She could not take the stress of the creditor calls when she became late. She sought relief in Chapter 7.

You file bankruptcy because you want a fresh start. The law allows you to keep assets that are necessary for you after bankruptcy. In addition, bankruptcy allows you to discharge certain debts that you have incurred, and you can begin the process of credit repair.

Most people file bankruptcy because an unforeseen event has occurred in their lives, nearly always outside of their control. Either one or both spouses have lost their job or had a decrease in their work hours. To afford to raise a family today with all the expenses involved, many families are on the edge at all times. If one spouse is out of work for a period of time, or even just one family member is unable to contribute, it's easy to get behind on the bills. The problem arises when you start using your credit cards for your living expenses, and you're unable to pay them in full when they come due. Most credit cards have high interest that will continue to accrue. And if you miss one payment or are late, many credit card companies automatically charge the default interest. They entice you with offers of low interest rates, balance transfers, and other promotions. Then all you do is skip a beat, and you're paying over a 30 percent interest rate. The next thing you know, you're behind on your mortgage because you can't keep all the bills current.

Other than loss of a job, what we see a lot of is people who have a medical condition—they're injured or they get sick—and their medical situation prevents them from being able to work. Sometimes their inability to work is temporary and sometimes it's permanent. Meanwhile, their obligations, such as car and mortgage payments and educational loans, begin to pile up, making it very difficult to pay back the creditors at that point.

In the event of a divorce, the husband's and wife's earnings are no longer combined and their expenses no longer split. An individual income may not be enough to live on in addition to paying child support and alimony, and the spouse who has custody of the children may not have enough income to provide the extras. Marital debts that may have accumulated now have to be split in addition to the added expense of living alone. So a divorce can wreak havoc on family finances. Bankruptcy is a good option.

Another reason to consider filing bankruptcy is involvement with a business that fails. The American dream is to have your own part-time or full-time business. Often, the dream doesn't work out. Either the local economy doesn't support your business, or the product you sell or the service you provide doesn't succeed despite your hard work. Many times, a business failure will have the effect of pulling you down individually. Even though they're business debts, you may be obligated personally to the creditors or on loans to the bank, and because of the business failure, the creditors will come after you personally.

Another prevalent reason for filing bankruptcy concerns the elderly. They're no longer able to stay employed due to their age, and they go from working full time to living on Social Security. The Social Security check isn't enough to cover all their expenses, and they get caught incurring credit card debt.

For those in financial trouble, bankruptcy still remains a good option because you're getting a fresh start. There are loan consolidation programs and debt settlement opportunities available. If you are exploring these options, look closely at the fees these options charge, as well as the total amount of money you're going to have to pay back. It may shock you.

Debt consolidators don't have the ability to fight lawsuits brought on by creditors. If the creditor doesn't want to participate in their program and decides to come after you, you will have to defend yourself in court. If you decide to go the debt settlement route, you will need cash to settle those debts. Debts typically settle for between 20 percent and 80 percent of the current balance, which includes the accrued interest.

What are the requirements for filing bankruptcy?

Melissa worked two jobs but was unable to keep her spending under control, and her credit cards got out of hand. Once she took the debtor education courses and obtained her discharge, she set up a budget and was able to live within her means.

Adam wanted to get married and start a new life without bringing his debt with him. He was able to file and receive his discharge in ninety days from start to finish.

Prior to filing for bankruptcy, the law requires you to take a debtor education course. The course is online and takes approximately an hour. After you file, you must take a financial management course, which is also online and around an hour long.

In these courses, you'll learn how to budget your money and hopefully not fall into the same situation you got yourself into before. These courses became required in 2005 when creditors were noticing repeat filers and debtors who were not making any attempt to repay them, despite having a decent income. So Congress changed the rules. People have told me that the courses are actually interesting and that they've benefited from them going forward.

Generally, the time-consuming part is locating all your creditor information and completing the checklist of items that you'll need. If you work with an attorney, he or she will give you a checklist of documents that you'll need to put together, including tax returns, pay stubs, a Kelly Blue Book valuation on your automobile, and a Zillow valuation on your house. You'll also be required to take the credit-counseling course and prepare a budget of income and expenses. Bankruptcy attorneys will require all fees to be paid prior to filing your case. Our office works out a payment plan to get the process started and manage your creditors. After you assemble all of your documents and deliver them to your attorney, Chapter 7 will take approximately ninety days to obtain a discharge once it is filed. In a Chapter 13, it takes typically three or five years to receive a discharge.

Do I qualify for bankruptcy and how long does it take?

Michael was a physician who was juggling pay-ments to an ex-wife and the IRS, as well as signifi-cant credit card debt incurred helping educate his kids. He had a good income, but the interest and penalties on the debt were significant, and he was left with with little for living expenses. He was able to file Chapter 13 and stop all interest and penal-ties. He was then able to pay off the debt he owed.

Almost everybody qualifies for some type of bankruptcy, whether it is Chapter 7 or Chapter 13. A Chapter 7 is a liquidation where all debt is wiped out with a few exceptions (e.g., student loans), and Chapter 13 is considered a reorganization bankruptcy where you pay some or all of your debts back over time. Two factors will determine which chapter you file. The first is the assets you have and whether they are exempt. The second qualification is analyzing whether your family is above or below median income. All income sources are considered, including rent that you might be receiving from a family member.

In 2005, the bankruptcy laws were amended fol-lowing efforts from credit card companies to pres-sure individuals making above a certain annual income to pay some or all of their creditors back in

Chapter 13. Congress amended the code to include the means test, which, depending on the state you live in and your family size, will determine whether or not you would qualify for Chapter 7. Massachusetts has one of the highest median incomes in the country. The median income for a single person living in the state in 2014 was $55,611; the median income for a family of two was $70,588; and median income for a family of four was $106,841.

Occasionally, even if you're above the median income, you still can qualify for Chapter 7 if you have greater-than-average deductions such as union dues, health insurance, and a higher-than-average mortgage or auto payment. These deductions would allow you to offset some of that additional income. In determining whether or not you qualify for filing Chapter 7 bankruptcy, there are other factors that should be considered. If someone has recently died in your family and you are due to get an inheritance, the money you're going to inherit could go to pay your creditors. Also, a personal injury may not be fully exempt from creditors in a Chapter 7 bankruptcy.

In addition, you're only able to file for bankruptcy under Chapter 7 every eight years after receiving your last discharge, while a Chapter 13 allows you to file every four years. This law was changed in 2005.

At the outset, your attorney will calculate the means test and perform an analysis of your assets and exemptions; then you will take credit counseling. Once you've made your final decision, you are ready to complete the process. A bankruptcy petition, schedules, and a statement of financial affairs are filed with the court.

After you file for bankruptcy, you will have to appear for what's commonly called a *meeting of creditors* or a *341 meeting*. It will generally be held within an hour's drive from where you live. Prior to the hearing, your attorney will provide the trustee with pay stubs and tax returns.

The 341 hearings are conducted by the trustee, who will ask you if you've listed all of your assets and liabilities on the schedules, whether your schedules were true and accurate at the time you filed for bankruptcy, and whether the schedules are still true and accurate at the time of the meeting. If you've forgotten or deliberately failed to list all of your real estate assets, chances are the trustee would have done his research and already know that. If you've listed all your assets and all your liabilities and your assets are exempt, the trustee will close out your case and file a no-asset report with the court.

By law, you're not entitled to receive a discharge for sixty days after the 341 meeting. The sixty-day period is generally for any creditors to object to your discharge. This rarely happens unless you have abused your cards prior to filing.

After sixty days, the bankruptcy clerk will mail you an *order of discharge*. This is endorsed by the judge and states that your debts have been discharged. There are no tax consequences to receiving a discharge in bankruptcy, unlike a debt being written off by a creditor. Furthermore, the whole process from start to finish will have taken approximately ninety days.

If you file for Chapter 13, the bankruptcy process takes a little longer. The initial phase of filing, meeting with the trustee, and resolving any objections with the trustee and creditors takes approximately six months.

Another prerequisite of filing bankruptcy is to determine whether or not you've transferred any property in the last four years (or in the last ten if it's a self-settled trust). Many people run into trouble with creditors and start transferring property to a spouse or a family member, and they transfer it for less than the actual value so it's outside the reach of creditors. The bankruptcy laws frown on these types of transfers. They're considered civilly fraudulent and can be voided for the benefit of creditors.

When you meet with your bankruptcy attorney, you'll want to make sure to tell them of any transfers you made in the last few years or to yourself under another entity; they may be able to be fixed.

Who finds out about my bankruptcy filing?

Sandra worked in customer service at a bank and was terrified that she would lose her job. Since there is no requirement in the bankruptcy code to notify your employer, she was able to complete her bankruptcy, and her employer never found out.

Other than your individual creditors, the only entities that find out about you filing a bankruptcy are the three credit reporting agencies: TransUnion, Experian, and Equifax. Your employer does not get a notice. Your spouse will not find out unless you tell him or her or if he or she sees your mail, and your spouse does not have to consent to your filing. It will not appear in the local newspaper. You can't even find out if someone filed by using a Google search. Word just doesn't get around. Yes, a bankruptcy is recorded in the public record, but it isn't published for the average person to see. So don't worry.

Bankruptcy And Your Home

If I file bankruptcy, will I lose my house?

Other than a ten-year-old car, William's only asset was his home of thirty years, and he had paid down most of his mortgage. He was able to file bankruptcy and eliminate his credit card and medical debt. His house was protected in the process, and he was able keep current on his mortgage.

Not if you don't want to. If you are current on your mortgage, and you don't owe more than what your home is worth, you can enter and exit bankruptcy with your home and mortgage intact. If you aren't current on your mortgage, you have other options. We'll have more on this topic later.

Living in Massachusetts entitles you to the state's homestead exemption. If you haven't already, you'll need to fill out a simple document available online or by having your attorney prepare it and record it at the registry of deeds. Your lawyer can help you. A homestead protects the equity in your house up to $500,000, meaning after your mortgage is deducted from the value, you have equity in your home. So if you own a $300,000 house and you owe $200,000, your $100,000 in equity would be protected under the Massachusetts homestead exemption. This is one of the most liberal homestead exemptions in the country.

Massachusetts also has an automatic homestead exemption. If for some reason you do not have a homestead exemption filed, you still get to exempt up to $125,000 in your home. So you could still be able to file bankruptcy and protect your home if you had less than $125,000 in equity.

How can I keep my home if I am having trouble affording it?

Joseph was diagnosed with cancer and was unable to continue working while in treatment. A year later, he had beaten the cancer and was employed again but found himself eight months behind on his mortgage and with a pile of credit card debt. He filed Chapter 13 and is paying his delinquent mortgage payments over five years.

Keeping your home obviously means that you're going to have to pay for your home. Just because you're receiving a discharge of bankruptcy doesn't mean that the bank is going to wipe out your mortgage or that you're not going to have to make your regular monthly mortgage payments. During the process, the lender is still going to be expecting you to make the payments, and if you don't make the payments, the lender will foreclose on you. It's as simple as that. Otherwise, you'll be able to exit your bankruptcy and keep your home.

If you aren't current on your mortgage and are having trouble catching up, you can file a Chapter 13 and pay your mortgage arrears a little each month over sixty months. In the meantime, if you stay current and make your payments, the bank can't foreclose on you, whether it wants to or not. The law doesn't allow it. I regularly see people who haven't made mortgage payments in months or years, and they are able to catch up with affordable monthly payments in Chapter 13.

Now, let's say you want to keep your house, but you can't afford the monthly payments. Your other option is to try to modify your loan. If you are approved, the bank could reduce your current interest rate and put the delinquent payments on the back end of the loan. Then you'll just resume payments under what is generally a trial modification. There are quite a few government programs as well as in-house modifications that banks are willing to look at to keep you in your home. The programs depend on whether you're current or delinquent on your mortgage. Modifications are going to require a financial hardship, such as one resulting from a divorce, illness, loss of job, or cut in work hours.

The guidelines on getting approved are tricky, especially if you are self-employed. As part of our prebankruptcy planning or foreclosure defense, our office assists individuals and families in modifying their loans when appropriate. There is also assistance available with the local housing authorities.

If you can't modify, you're left with only Chapter 13 if you want to keep the house. Let's assume for a moment that you are behind six mortgage payments of $2,000 per month for a total of $12,000, and no matter how hard you try, you're not able to get current. You're getting letters from the bank saying you're delinquent. You have the ability to file for Chapter 13 and pay the balance over time.

Let's break it down further. For example, in a Chapter 13, your payment will be approximately $225 a month for sixty months, meaning that each and every month for the next five years, you will mail a check for $225 to the bankruptcy trustee. After the 10 percent trustee fee is deducted, the balance will be sent to your bank.

When you are under the protection of Chapter 13, the bank cannot foreclose on you as long as you're paying your trustee payment of $225 and keeping your mortgage current.

Sometimes in Chapter 13, despite your best efforts, you're not going to be able to afford the current payments plus the trustee payments. If that happens, you have to take a hard look at your situation and see whether keeping this home is in your best interest.

Part of your plan might be to file the Chapter 13 and continue the effort to modify your loan or struggle to pay the arrears over the life of the plan. If you're unable to do afford it, you can sell the property in Chapter 13 or convert to a Chapter 7 to discharge your other creditors rather quickly. That's not something that you hope to do, but reality may be at the door. You will be able to sell your house while in Chapter 13.

When you are trying to save your house, one of the many benefits of bankruptcy is that you get what's called the *automatic stay*. Now, let's assume that your bank is putting pressure on you and begins foreclosure proceedings. It may start with a simple form letter. But the bank may get more serious and hire an attorney, send you a formal letter, file a proceeding in court, publish the notice in the newspaper, and schedule an auction date.

When you file for bankruptcy, the court imposes the automatic stay. The stay means that all foreclosure and collection activity stops at the moment of filing. If your intention is to keep your home and you file Chapter 13, the automatic stay allows you time to submit a plan to the bankruptcy court, in which you would state that you intend to keep the property and resume payments.

What are my options if I don't want my house or can't afford it?

Jeffrey came to us having recently divorced and being unable to sell the marital home, which was worth less than what was owed. He wanted to get a fresh start and not have the bank come after him for the difference after a foreclosure. He was able to file bankruptcy, and he discharged his obligation to the bank.

Let's say you can't afford your monthly payments or that your house is underwater; in other words, you owe more on it than what it's worth. You have the option to walk away or abandon your house. By abandoning the house, you receive a discharge in bankruptcy relieving you from your obligation to the bank, whether you have one mortgage or two mortgages. You also can sell the home by short sale or give it back to the bank in what is called a *deed in lieu of foreclosure* (hand the bank the keys) and release yourself from obligation. Your personal liability is discharged in bankruptcy, and the bank can't come after you for the deficiency.

Here is an example. Without bankruptcy, if you have a house worth $350,000 and owe $400,000, you are underwater. The bank sells the house at a foreclosure auction for $300,000. You would be liable for the remaining $100,000. A bankruptcy, though, would eliminate that liability. It's all part of the fresh start bankruptcy affords you. If you decide not to file for bankruptcy, the bank can come after you for the difference. If the bank forecloses and decides to sue you, it has twenty years to collect on the judgment. You run a risk by not filing bankruptcy that the deficiency judgment will hang over your head for up to twenty years.

How does Chapter 13 work?

Susan and Ed had well-paying jobs, but unfortunately in maintaining all of their children's activities and paying for day care for the youngest, they had accumulated a lot of credit card debt. They were able to file Chapter 13 and pay a nominal amount to the creditors each month through the bankruptcy plan.

The Chapter 13 plan is based on your current income and expenses. It is essentially a budget that shows where your monthly income is coming from and where it's going to in itemized expenses. The plan has to be approved by the trustee for feasibility to make sure that your income and expenses are reasonable. If the trustee signs off on the plan, then it goes to the judge, who—assuming there's no objection from any creditors—will approve your plan.

Once the judge approves your plan, the payment that you make remains fixed for five years. Now, if you have a significant increase in your income, you may be required to make a larger plan payment to your creditors.

We talked earlier about assets that you will be able to keep in Chapter 7. In Chapter 13, you have the ability to keep the luxury items or assets that are nonexempt in Chapter 7, such as boats, personal business assets, and certain securities. Retirement funds are covered or protected as an exempt asset. But those other assets that are not necessary to your daily life are considered nonexempt assets. While you will be able to keep these assets, you will be required to pay the value of those assets to your creditors over the life of the Chapter 13 plan.

For example, if the value of a boat you had was, say, $18,000, you could deduct $12,000 for the allowable exemption in both Chapter 7 and Chapter 13. The remaining $6,000, which is not exempt, would be paid to the creditors through the Chapter 13 plan, so your payment would be approximately $115 a month for the next five years. That payment would go to the bankruptcy trustee who would divide it proportionally among your creditors.

You also have the option while in Chapter 13 to attempt to modify your home loan again. If you were denied your loan modification before you filed for Chapter 13, and there's a change in circumstances, you can modify your loan in Chapter 13.

We have helped many people obtain a loan modification while in Chapter 13. You always have that option. When you are behind on your payments and file for bankruptcy because you don't want to lose your house, and subsequently you're able to modify your mortgage, you can then exit Chapter 13 by dismissing the case or converting to Chapter 7 if you have other creditors.

Can I eliminate home equity loans or second mortgages in bankruptcy?

Stephanie and her husband bought a house in 2006 during the height of the real estate market with what was called an 80/20 loan, *in which there was a second mortgage for 20 percent of the purchase price. The value of their house had now fallen below the amount they owed on their first mortgage, and their house was significantly underwater. They were able to file a Chapter 13 and discharge their second mortgage.*

Another benefit of filing Chapter 13 in Massachusetts is that you're able to strip your second mortgage if the value of the house is less than what you owe on your first mortgage.

For example, if your house is worth $300,000, and you have a first mortgage with a balance of $310,000 as well as a second mortgage of $90,000, the value of your house is less than your first mortgage. Therefore, in Chapter 13, you could strip the second mortgage (the $90,000 mortgage) from your property. In fact, you will get an order from the court after you've completed Chapter 13 that will be recorded with the registry of deeds showing the mortgage is discharged. This helps families who bought homes back in the mid-2000s at the height of the market and then saw the market fall out. When the market crashed, the value of those houses plummeted below their original purchase prices.

This option is not available if you have equity in your house or if the value of your home is greater than your first mortgage. So it comes with conditions.

What happens to liens that are on my house?

Tanya wanted to sell her house but was unable to because she had liens from credit card companies that had obtained judgments. We filed Chapter 7 for her and removed the liens as part of the ninety-day process. She was able to sell her house and keep the proceeds.

If over the years you have been unable to pay your creditors and they've put liens on your home, you are going to be able to discharge those liens in bankruptcy. To the extent that you have a home-stead, you will be able to strip the liens in bank-ruptcy. Your attorney will file what's called a *motion to avoid* the lien with the bankruptcy court. Only judicial liens, which are liens obtained by lawsuits against you by creditors, can be stripped. It Liens that cannot be stripped include any liens from the IRS or the department of revenue or any liens for domestic support obligations, such as child sup-port and alimony. If you owe child support and maintenance payments, those debts are not dis-chargeable, and those debts can be enforced with a lien on your property. If you have liens on a house that's underwater and you intend to abandon the property, there is no reason to remove the liens. When the senior mortgage, or first mortgage, goes through the foreclosing process, the liens that are behind it will be wiped out. So you do not have to worry about having to deal with those liens if the property was foreclosed on, as long as you list the underlying debt in your bankruptcy.

Will I get to keep my other assets in bankruptcy, such as my car and household possessions?

Jose came to us with a mountain of credit debt, but he was most afraid of losing his Harley if he filed a Chapter 7. We were able to exempt the Harley using the "wild card" exemption, and he was able to file Chapter 7 and keep the motorcycle.

The short answer is yes. Again, the idea behind filing bankruptcy is to give you a fresh start and allow you to keep your necessary possessions: house, car, furniture, jewelry, clothes, lawn mower, dog—all those items of value that most people need in life. There's a limit on what the value of these items can be worth. Like the homestead, these are called *exemptions*. The value of these items has to be reasonable and is further defined in the code; you may not be able to keep luxury items. So you get to keep your car, but it's not going to be a brand-new Mercedes with no loan on it. It's going to be your basic automobile, along with reasonable retirement accounts and personal possessions.

If you want to keep a luxury item—say a boat, a motorcycle, or a camper—you may be able to keep it under what is called the *wild card exemption*. A wild card exemption is possession of one or more items with a value of up to approximately

$12,000. In your life you may not consider these luxury items. I've had more than a few people tell me that a Harley is a necessity.

If your luxury item has a value greater than $12,000, and you still want to file for Chapter 7, the trustee will take that item and sell it. The trustee will give you up to the $12,000 you have exempted. The rest of the proceeds are used to pay your creditors. That's how Chapter 7 works. Generally, if you have those types of assets, you will do some type of prebankruptcy planning. You may want to consider selling the asset prior to filing for Chapter 7, spend the money on living expenses, and keep the difference. And you always have the option of filing for Chapter 13 and keeping the asset.

Bankruptcy And Debt

What debts are discharged in bankruptcy?

Kevin owed the IRS for old taxes and was discouraged that they kept adding penalties and interest to an amount that he couldn't afford. They had levied his bank account and were keeping his tax refund every year. He filed Chapter 7 and eliminated his old tax debt. He was able to begin receiving his tax refund immediately.

The short answer is unsecured debt and promises to pay. Those are credit cards that are either current, delinquent, or sold off to a collection agency for failure to pay the original creditor. Credit card debt is freely traded as a commodity. The initial credit card company, once it has tired of chasing you around for the debt, will sell your debt to another collection agency. Then you'll start receiving calls from the new company. When it gets tired of you, or maybe you have moved or changed your number, that company will sell your debt off to a third agency, then to a fourth agency, and down the line. If you've been delinquent over the years for not making credit card payments, you're liable to hear from a collection agency you haven't heard from before out of the blue. So it's important when you file for bankruptcy that not only the underlying creditor is listed but also the agencies that are bothering you, so they receive notice. Now, you may have thrown out your mail by this point or not know who's out there, but a lot of this information will appear on your credit report. And if it doesn't show up, what's most important is that the initial creditor is listed. So if your MasterCard is on your bankruptcy petition, even though it has sold it off two or three times down the road, the debt will be discharged.

Unsecured debt is debt for which there's no security, security being a house, car, jewelry, or furniture that you've given as collateral for the loan. You'll get a complete discharge from all of the credit card debts as long as you don't abuse the credit cards in the three months prior to filing. The law says that if you abuse those cards during that time by buying luxury items or getting cash advances against those cards, those specific debts will not be dischargeable in bankruptcy.

It's important to work with your bankruptcy attorney to review the activity on your credit cards in the time leading up to the filing. If you do have those types of charges on your cards, sometimes it's advisable to wait a little bit to file the bankruptcy and let those charges get further from the filing date, outside of that three-month period. However, intent is always a problem, even if you are outside of the three months. There's a presumption that if you file for bankruptcy within three months of using the card for a luxury item or cash advance, that you did it intentionally—

you went to Best Buy and bought that TV with no intention of paying it back. And that's considered obvious.

Mortgage debt and car loans are not discharged in bankruptcy. Your personal guarantee to these lenders, though, is discharged. So if you're not making a mortgage or a car payment on time, they can't come after you for the difference if you default. They can still take the item and foreclose or repossess, but you'll be discharged of the personal obligation.

Student loans, as I'm sure you have heard, are not dischargeable. When Congress enacted the student loan laws, it decided to give you the money to educate your children or yourself, but it wants the money back, unless there's a hardship.

Generally, a hardship is a physical or mental handicap that would not allow you to repay the loans. And essentially you have to be pretty much on or below the poverty line to get that hardship. If you have any ability to pay your loan back, Congress is not going to let you walk away from it.

You'll be discharged from utility bills owed to both public and private companies. They will reset your meter to zero after the filing date. Therefore, if you owe the electric or gas company, you'll get a fresh start. Public utility companies will service you in the future and wipe out the old balance. However, if you owe a private company and list it on your bankruptcy schedules, the debt will be discharged, but that company may choose to not sell you oil in the future.

You can also discharge all kinds of medical debt that you have, whether it be copays or the actual bill. You can also discharge court judgments. You may have been taken to court or sued by creditors, and they have a judgment against you and bring you back to court; those debts also are discharged in bankruptcy. After you file, your bankruptcy attorney will send a "suggestion of bankruptcy" to the court, and you will no longer need to appear in court.

What debts survive bankruptcy?

Missy had significant student debt that she was unable to pay monthly, as she had so much other debt. She was able to file Chapter 7 and discharge her old utility, medical, and credit card debt. She was then able to start paying off her student loans regularly.

Student loans survive as well as your car loan, mortgage, and domestic support obligations. The automatic stay allows you to suspend payments on student loans while you're in bankruptcy. So for approximately ninety days, you won't have Sallie Mae contacting you. However, once you receive your discharge in bankruptcy, you'll have to go back to making the student loan payments and keeping current. Any nondischargeable tax debt survives too. The rule of thumb is the last three years, subject to the exemptions discussed in the section on taxes.

When will the creditors stop calling?

Gloria was living on Social Security and received daily and nightly phone calls from collection agencies for debts she had incurred by helping out her grandchildren. These calls were causing her tremendous stress, as she was trying to send them something each month. She filed Chapter 7, and the calls stopped. She was able to stretch her monthly budget to make it work.

Legally, creditors can call up until you've actually filed a bankruptcy. Once the case is filed and the creditors are on the schedules, the clerk of the bankruptcy court will mail them a notice of your filing. It will take about a week after you file until those notices are mailed out. Once the creditors receive the notice, they are required by law to stop calling. However, until they actually become aware of the bankruptcy, they'll keep contacting you. One thing you can do if they call you after you've filed is to give them your bankruptcy case number, and that'll be the end of it.

Living in Massachusetts, you get an added benefit: if you're represented by an attorney during prebankruptcy, the creditors can't contact you. If you retain a law firm to represent you in bankruptcy, you want to make sure that before filing, you have an arrangement with the firm in which it will field the credit calls prior to you filing. For the most part, credit card companies and collection companies are aware that they can't contact you after you file. It's a rare case when creditors call after they've been notified. Sometimes there may be private vendors or creditors—for example, a builder or business owner—who aren't used to having somebody list them in a bankruptcy petition. So you may get calls from creditors like that, but your attorney should be able to put a stop to them if the calls continue.

Also, at the time you file, if you're subject to a wage garnishment by a creditor, the IRS, or the Massachusetts Department of Revenue, that will stop also. When you file, you or your attorney will want to fax a copy to your bank and to the creditor so the wage garnishment will stop, whether it's from the IRS, the department of revenue, or another creditor. By law they have to stop.

In Massachusetts, if you don't pay your taxes to the department of revenue, at some point the department will take away your driver's license. The revenue department has no mercy. If this has happened to you, all you need to do is go down to the registry of motor vehicles with a copy of the bankruptcy petition, and your license will be reinstated at that time.

In addition, if you're on a payment plan with the IRS or the department of revenue at the time you file bankruptcy, you will stop making those payments. At that point, if the taxes are discharged through Chapter 7, you'll never have to make another payment again. If the tax is not discharged, you'll be able to resume payments upon the completion of your Chapter 7, which will be in approximately three to four months. If you decide to file a Chapter 13, you will pay those taxes that are not dischargeable over sixty months.

Can I keep a credit card after I file for bankruptcy?

Mark was disappointed that all of his credit cards were canceled immediately on filing bankruptcy, especially because he lost his beloved AMEX card that he'd had for years. He was surprised that he was able to qualify for a new credit card within two months of filing. It was only a small-balance card, but he was able to rebuild his credit back into the 700s from that one card.

Many individuals have credit cards that they've had for years, and they've become very attached to them, whether it is their Gap, Old Navy, or Macy's card. When they've used them, they always paid them off on time. The question always is, can I keep that card? Well, first of all, if you pay it off on time, you don't have to list it on your bankruptcy form, so it doesn't even have to appear on your schedules. If your Gap card has a zero balance, the company will not get notification that you filed for bankruptcy through the bankruptcy court.

However, the entire credit world is connected. So Gap would ultimately find out, whether through some type of service the company subscribes to or when it routinely runs your credit. So what will the retailer do when it finds out? It's a possibility that Gap could cancel your card. That is why it's important that you rebuild your credit after you file. Even if you lose that beloved store card that you have had for years, by filing bankruptcy you will be able to obtain new cards right away. That's for cards with a zero balance.

How about those cards that have a balance, but you still want to keep them, and yet you don't want to list them in your bankruptcy? Well, first of all, you're going to be signing a document certifying that you disclosed all of your assets and all of your liabilities. This means that you are required to list it. That should be enough of a reason.

But if for some reason you inadvertently forgot to list a card with a balance, the credit card company again would most likely find out that you had filed for bankruptcy. This is a problem after you file, because if the creditor is not listed as a creditor, you will not receive a discharge from that credit card.

So now you're in the position where the credit card company has canceled your card, but you have a balance due to them, yet the balance is not discharged in bankruptcy. If you can catch this mistake early on, you can amend your schedules to include that creditor. But if it's a year or even a few months after your case is closed, you will have to reopen your case and add the creditor at that time. That's an additional expense to you which may even be greater than what you owe on the card. However, having the card shown as a charge off on your credit report after you file bankruptcy is certainly not something you want. So it's very important that you list all of your creditors initially. When your attorney downloads all of your credit reports prior to filing, he will pick up on whom you owe anyway. So a card with a balance shouldn't be missed.

As far as your credit reports go, as you know, not all of your creditors report to the credit bureau. For instance, hospitals, doctors, utilities, cell phone companies, and similar types of creditors don't always report. This is another important reason to list them, so they don't sue you later on and it becomes part of your credit report as a judgment.

How will my credit be affected by filing bankruptcy?

Maria came to us having been recently divorced. Her credit score was so low that she wasn't able to obtain a loan to replace her fifteen-year-old car, which was breaking down constantly. She had left-over debt from the divorce that was being reported negatively. We were able to file a Chapter 7, wipe out her debt, and reset her credit score at 680 within a few months.

The chances are if you're reading this book, you're already having trouble paying your creditors. Maybe you've missed a few payments, have a court judgment against you, or have maxed out your credit cards. All of these factors have already contributed to your credit score being affected negatively. Collectively, these little nicks and bruises have caused your credit score to fall.

As you know, the entire credit world is connected in the age of the Internet. Credit card companies are finding out from other companies whether you're current on your payments. This may have already resulted in your credit limits being cut on your cards.

Now, ordinarily these delinquencies will stay in your report for six years if you do not file bankruptcy. Filing bankruptcy cures the negative reporting faster. The three credit reporting bureaus are TransUnion, Equifax, and Experian. All are subject to the Fair Debt and Credit Reporting Act. This act states that individuals who have filed bankruptcy are not subject to negative reporting from credit card and collection agencies after receiving their discharge. The good news is that the credit card companies don't have a choice in this. This is a law, and so all their negative reporting of you for all these years is going to stop, and you'll get that fresh start on your credit. Essentially this has the effect of being *credit neutral*, meaning that a credit card company's report is no longer a black mark, but it isn't positive either.

Obviously, the fact that you filed for bankruptcy stays on your credit report for a period of time. However, from what we've seen, generally it takes only about two years after you receive your discharge before there is no negative impact on your ability to borrow money. There's also an entire cottage industry of credit card companies that will solicit you subsequent to bankruptcy. Your mailbox will be stuffed with preapproved applications. Upon receipt of the discharge, you should take advantage of those offers. That's how you rebuild your score.

Generally, we see credit scores reset at between 650 and 680 immediately following the bankruptcy, and this may be higher than the score you have before you file. But in order to get your score back up in the 700s, you're going to have to take affirmative steps to rebuild your credit. It doesn't happen on its own.

Take advantage of those small offers that come your way for a $500 Capital One card or a MasterCard. Some of these offers may be for a secured card. To become a good credit card borrower, buy groceries and gas and pay the balance on time. Don't max out the card and try to pay it off, or most of it, each month. By doing this, you will rebuild your score.

Also, if you make credit card payments faithfully, you'll find that companies will raise your credit limits as you go along. All of these things are going to be important for you in obtaining your fresh start and rebuilding.

You will find that in order to buy a house, there's a twenty-four-month waiting period prior to being able to get a conventional, an or any other type of mortgage. You also may not get the preferred rate for a car loan for two years after your bankruptcy discharge. But these waiting periods after bankruptcy are often far better than if you had done nothing.

You may think, "Why would a credit card company send me a new credit card? Why would they want my business?" Prior to filing bankruptcy, you have all this debt. You're not a good credit risk because you have all kinds of payments that you can't make and balances on credit cards that you can't afford to reduce. A new card is probably the last thing you need in any event, unless you want to prolong the inevitable.

However, after you've completed your bankruptcy, you no longer have that financial burden—credit card balances are no longer weighing on your score and impacting your ability to make payments. So you truly have a fresh start. The credit card companies know it and are more than happy to send you a new card and start making money off of you again. But now you not only have the ability to pay on time because you've gotten a reduction in your debt, but also you have an incentive to pay: you want to get your fresh start, and you're not going to go back to where you came from again.

The other reason why credit card companies are willing to give you credit cards after you file is that you're not going to be able to file Chapter 7 again for eight years. So now that you have received a bankruptcy discharge and have that new Capital One card for $500, if you don't pay it off, the company will now have eight years to go after you to collect. And you're not going to be able to file bankruptcy again, so that gives them eight years to harass you.

Filing a bankruptcy does not affect your debit card. So if you feel that you don't want to be using credit cards again, you certainly have the use of your debit card. But your debit card, as well as prepaid credit cards, does not report at all to the credit bureaus, so you're not going to rebuild that credit again.

If you're young enough and you're going to want to buy another house or a car at some point in the future, you definitely need to get back in the credit world. You'll want to take advantage of credit cards that actually report to the credit bureaus. You need to actually obtain credit in order to have it reflect positively on your score.

Let's take a moment to discuss what happens if you're going to be applying for student loans, which is a question I encounter all of the time. If you have children in college or getting ready to apply, there are federal student loan programs out there for both students and their parents. The parents will obtain what's called a *Parent PLUS loan* or will be cosigners on their children's loans. Your credit score might already be to a point where you don't qualify for Parent PLUS loans anyway, so your children will be forced to obtain the loans by themselves. And by filing for bankruptcy, you may be denied these loans.

However, your children should be able to receive additional loans as a result of your poor credit. There are many opportunities for children whose parents are unable to help them with their education. So your children will be able to obtain student loans, whether federal or private, without your assistance to get an education. At that point you can make an arrangement with your children to make payments on their student loans if you wish to help them out in years to come. As part of the prebankruptcy planning, your attorney will review your credit reports with you.

Our office has a program in which, forty-five days after receiving your discharge, you'll receive a copy of your credit report to see the impact of the bankruptcy on the individual creditors who were reporting negatively to make sure that those negative comments are now off of the report. In addition, the service will monitor your credit for up to a year, making sure that you're not getting unfavorable comments and are able to rebuild your credit by obtaining new credit cards.

The good news about repairing your credit is that there's a set of consumer protection laws that work to your advantage. These laws are not discretionary. The bank and credit card companies can't just decide to report negatively against you after you file for bankruptcy. The federal laws protect this from happening. And based upon experience, I can say that it's a rare instance when a discrepancy appears on a credit report subsequent to bankruptcy for a debt that was discharged.

How will my cosigner be affected?

Sarah had significant tax and credit card debt, but she was most concerned about her father being affected, as he had cosigned her car loan. Sarah was not delinquent on the payments and wanted to keep the car. She was able to file bankruptcy, her father's credit was protected, and Sarah was able to keep the car.

Along with the topic of credit, another question that comes up is, What happens if my mother or my father or my spouse cosigned a loan for me? Will it affect my cosigner's credit? The answer is no as long as you continue to make your payments on time. If you have a car with a loan that was cosigned by a parent or a spouse or other family member, it's important to continue to make those payments even though it will no longer appear as favorable or negative on your credit report, as these payments will appear on your family member's report. Your bankruptcy filing doesn't affect the cosigner's credit unless you don't make the payments on time, at which point it would affect them. Therefore, it's important to protect your cosigners by making sure you make your payments on time.

Conversely, if you cosigned a loan for a family member, but he or she is not making the payments on time causing your credit to be negatively affected, filing for bankruptcy will remove the negative reporting. That's the benefit of filing bankruptcy when family members have not honored their obligation to you by making timely payments.

Other Concerns

How does bankruptcy affect my spouse, or how is my spouse affected if I've been a plaintiff in a divorce?

Tiffany had racked up credit cards without telling her husband, and the minimum on the cards was consuming a large amount of her take-home pay each month. She came to us but was afraid to tell her husband. We were able to convince her husband that he would not be affected, and she was able to obtain a discharge in Chapter 7.

Bankruptcy affects him or her in that the family income must be counted in order to pay creditors. If your spouse makes a significant amount of money and the debts are in your name, unfortunately his or her income is going to be considered in the disposable income calculation, or the *means test*, which I'll explain later. However, your spouse's Social Security number is not listed on the petition, so the court doesn't recognize him or her. And the spouse doesn't sign anything. Therefore, your spouse's creditors would not be notified, and the fact that you filed bankruptcy would not appear on your husband's or your wife's credit report.

If all of the creditors are in your name alone and not your spouse's, you have the ability to file bankruptcy and wipe out your debt without affecting him or her. If your spouse is only an authorized user of the credit cards, he or she will not be responsible for the cards, and the debt would be discharged in bankruptcy. It's important to check both the husband's and wife's credit prior to filing bankruptcy to see who has the debt. A lot of times these credit card debts are old, and you may not remember or be wrong.

If you're separated from your spouse, your spouse's income does not come into play when calculating the means test. Only your income would come into play when determining whether or not you can afford to pay your debts back. You also do not need your spouse's permission to file bankruptcy. You can file it on your own whether your husband or wife allows you to or not; you're not required by law to get his or her consent.

The same goes for your home mortgage. If you were to file bankruptcy and your spouse did not, it would not appear on his or her credit report.

If you're divorced, alimony and child support are not dischargeable debts. If you're considerably in arrears with alimony or child support, and you're unable to work something out with your spouse or with the family court, you have the ability to file for Chapter 13. Then you can pay the arrears to your spouse over sixty months, similar to paying back old taxes or delinquent mortgage payments.

Another consideration in a divorce is if you're required to pay a property settlement pursuant to the divorce. For example, when you get divorced and are required to pay your former spouse $20,000 by a certain date, or you are required to pay his or her credit card debt or an amount of money upon the sale of a house, you can discharge that obligation in Chapter 13. It's certainly not going to make your former spouse happy, but the filing of a Chapter 13 bankruptcy trumps the divorce order.

We talked earlier about the automatic stay in that it stays all court proceedings. It does not, however, stay domestic support proceedings. If you and your former spouse are embroiled in a custody battle or trying to modify child support or alimony payments, those types of proceedings are not stayed in the bankruptcy action. The only actions that are stayed relating to your former spouse are those concerning any previous money owed for back support and the property settlements due to him or her.

Sometimes family court judges are not up to speed on bankruptcy laws. So you're going to want to make sure that your bankruptcy attorney speaks to your divorce lawyer and provides copies of any rules or applicable sections of the code that cover the intersection of your family matter with the bankruptcy.

This is really important because you don't want to be caught in a situation where the rights afforded you under the bankruptcy laws are not being followed through in the family court. Remember that bankruptcy is a federal protection; it's governed under federal laws, while divorce and family matters are governed under state laws.

Now, when it comes to making a decision as to whether one or both spouses file, again you're going to want to look at those credit reports to find out who owes the debt. If one spouse owes a significant amount of the debt and the other owes a very small portion, it certainly doesn't make sense to do a joint filing. Because if the spouse with the small amount of credit has made payments, he or she would be able to obtain student loans or better rates for car loans and mortgages should the need arise.

Obviously, the amount of debt that each spouse has is significant in deciding whether or not to do a joint filing or a single filing. If possible, you'll want to file a joint petition because you'll save on the cost of the attorney fees and only pay one filing fee.

Many times during a pending divorce, the divorce mediator or the attorneys for both parties will suggest that the bankruptcy be done prior to completing the divorce. This is advantageous because you'll enter the divorce agreement with no debt. Essentially, the marriage will end, and neither side will be saddled with debt they can't afford. Both of you start fresh and uncomplicated as your life moves forward.

If only one spouse decides to file but both are obligated on the credit card, the bankruptcy will discharge only one of the spouses. The creditor will be notified that one of the two, the husband or wife, has been discharged. But the credit card company will be free to pursue the other spouse. Thus, if one spouse decides to file, you'll want to consider that the other spouse will still be required to make payments on that credit card, or it will in fact affect the nonfiling spouse's credit.

How are taxes treated in bankruptcy?

Harold had lost his driver's license for failure to pay his state income tax. He filed bankruptcy, got his license back immediately, and eliminated his taxes in Chapter 7.

There are two basic rules for taxes in bankruptcy, and they are confusing. You really ought to consult a bankruptcy attorney on this, but here is the overview: there is a three-year rule and a two-year rule. Under the three-year rule, if the taxes were due more than three years ago, the debt will be discharged in bankruptcy. Under the two-year rule, those tax returns had to have been filed for at least two years.

For example, if the income tax is due from 2010, the tax would have been due on April 15, 2011, and three years from that date would be April 15, 2014. The 2010 tax debt would then be dischargeable any time after April 15, 2014. However, the two-year rule states that the tax return had to be filed for at least two years. So if you were on an extension or you were late, and you didn't file that return until, say, 2013, that would not have been two years and you'd have to wait until the two years were up before you could file for bankruptcy, even though the debt was older than three years.

Now, this rule gets a little tricky because there are some other exemptions too, and one is that any assessments on taxes have to be at least 240 days old. Also, in Massachusetts, state income taxes that were late-filed returns are not considered a filing, and there are issues with the dischargeability of that. So you want to consult with an attorney on a late filing.

Generally speaking, the IRS and the Massachusetts Department of Revenue are treated just like any other creditors in bankruptcy, although they may have a priority status. The automatic stay prevents them from garnishing or levying you while you're in bankruptcy. And they don't have any special powers. If you do decide to file for Chapter 13 because you have tax debt that is not dischargeable, the good news is that the penalties and late fees stop. All you're paying is essentially just the interest—which is currently a little over 3 percent—that will accrue during your case. The nondischargeable portion of your debt, which is generally any debt newer than three years, would be paid to the Chapter 13 trustee, and the trustee would make payments to the IRS or department of revenue. Again, there would be no garnishment, penalties, or late fees. Essentially, you're paying off the actual amount that you owed.

There are certain types of tax debt that are not dischargeable. If you were a business owner and owed what are commonly called 941 *taxes*, or payroll taxes, those taxes are not dischargeable in bankruptcy; nor are sales and meals taxes. If you're subject to any of those taxes, they're not dischargeable.

If the Social Security Administration or any other government agency somehow overpaid you by mistake, the debt that you owe back to them is also dischargeable.

Now, when it comes to making any determination of whether a debt is dischargeable or not, it's really important to get a copy of your tax transcripts before you file the case. Then, if there's any question that you may have some debt owed to the IRS or the department of revenue, you or your attorney can take a look at those tax transcripts before you file; you'll want to make sure that the tax debts are dischargeable at the date of filing. Sometimes you have to wait for a couple of months or even a year if you want to discharge those debts.

Sometimes prebankruptcy planning is needed to make sure that tax debts will fully discharge in bankruptcy. If the government has filed a notice of lien at the registry of deeds or the state or the IRS, the lien itself is not dischargeable in bankruptcy, so the lien will stay on your property. However, the lien has an expiration date. It's generally six years for the state and ten years for the IRS. Therefore, that lien would stay on your property until it expires. If the underlying debt is discharged in bankruptcy, however, the government can't renew its lien. Unfortunately, the lien does stay at least for that period of time.

Peter M. Daigle, Esq.

Are retirement accounts protected in bankruptcy?

Other than his car, Chuck's only significant asset was the $25,000 he had managed to save in an IRA. He was able to file Chapter 7 and protect the funds in the IRA.

Retirement accounts are called ERISA-qualified plans and include 401(k) plans, 403(b) plans, IRAs, and Roth IRAs. These are examples of retirement accounts that allow you to invest your pretax earnings and save for retirement. These accounts are protected in bankruptcy, as is any money due you from Social Security, veterans disability, or any type of government assistance.

Unfortunately, a lot of people come to us having already cashed in their retirement accounts to pay creditors. If they had come earlier, they would have been able to maintain their retirement accounts and eliminate the creditor debt that was strangling them. A tax penalty will occur on a withdrawal. Not only do you lose the money to pay the creditors, but you also are saddled with a tax from the IRS for cashing in retirement accounts early. So think twice about using retirement funds to pay creditors.

Conclusion

Hopefully, this book has cleared up some of the myths and mysteries about bankruptcy. Is bankruptcy right for you? Your instincts will tell you first. You'll now be more informed to make a decision. There is life after bankruptcy. Your credit will repair. You'll have disposable income to do things that you haven't been able to do in a long time—some may be necessities, or it may be something as simple as going out to lunch.

About the Author

Peter M. Daigle, Esq., is an attorney specializing in consumer bankruptcy. He has helped thousands of individuals and families obtain relief from creditors. The Daigle Law Office is located in Norwell and Centerville, Massachusetts, serving clients in Southeastern Massachusetts, Cape Cod, and the Islands. Peter lives on Cape Cod with his wife, Grace and has four children and two dogs. He is an avid outdoorsman, and his passions, aside from practicing law, include biking, skiing, and stand-up paddle boarding.

www.ingramcontent.com/pod-product-compliance
Lightning Source LLC
Chambersburg PA
CBHW070917180526
45168CB00005B/2043